MW00743417

SPEAKING
Of
Success

INSIGHT PUBLISHING
SEVIERVILLE, TENNESSEE

SPEAKING
Of
Success

Published by Insight Publishing Company
P.O. Box 4189
Sevierville, Tennessee 37864

10 9 8 7 6 5 4 3 2

Printed in the United States of America

ISBN-10: 1-60013-152-2
ISBN-13: 978-1-60013-2

Table of Contents

A Message from the Publisher

When we decided to do a series of books on success, we searched long and hard to find just the right combination of authors who were not only a success in business but were successful in their personal life as well.

The authors we found had personal stories to tell that revealed their inner values—values that contributed to the achievements they have made and the positive influence they have on others. These authors are people whom others revere as persons of integrity. They are winners.

Everyone wants to be a winner. I have never met anyone who wants to be a loser. And I'm sure you haven't either. That's why we found some of the best motivational/inspirational speakers and authors in the country to contribute to this series. Some of these men and women are household names. Others are rising stars. All of them have achieved the kind of success all of us want—the kind that sparks enthusiasm in others and leaves an indelible, positive impression.

The road to success is one of hard work and persistence. *Speaking of Success* can help you unlock your potential and inspire you to realize the many possibilities awaiting you as you learn how to remove any mental blocks you might have to the success you deserve.

If you're already well on your way down the success highway, the stories and experiences of these authors will encourage you, inform you, and I guarantee that you will learn something.

It is with great pride that we Insight Publishing present this series, *Speaking of Success.* We think you will discover that you will find something new each time you read through these books.

The chapters in this series are real page-turners, so get ready to be inspired. Get ready to be delighted. Get ready to learn. And remember, *you* are the author of your own success journey. Others can shine a light on the path but you must do the walking.

Interviews conducted by:
David E. Wright
President, International Speakers Network

Chapter 1

MONICA WOFFORD

David Wright (Wright)

Monica Wofford is a nationally acclaimed speaker, author, trainer, and leadership expert with more than seventeen years of experience. She has written, among other books, *Contagious Leadership,* which was complimented by Vice President Dick Cheney. Her areas of expertise include Leadership and Success, both being achieved with intention and on purpose. Corporations often call on Monica to rescue their managers from the deep end of the corporate pool when all they were given was a promotion and a life jacket but no new leadership skills. Monica's speaking and training career began back in 1989 and has taken her to all fifty states and several countries. She is known for engaging audiences and helping them make radical shifts in the behavior that creates successful leaders, whether of their own lives or the lives of others. Monica's customized training produces long-lasting results in the leadership of employees, customers, and even the voices in your head!

What is so important about leading the voices in one's head?

Monica Wofford (Wofford)

That's a good question and before I answer, I must first get you to admit that you have voices in your head, David. Do you talk to yourself? (Of course, he does!)

The voices in your head dictate behavior and actions and more importantly, the perceptions you have. Once these perceptions are made, and held on to, they become beliefs and we act on them. So if the voices are misleading us, then they might not be serving us well. You see, the voices in your head are a result of your confidence level or the belief that you can do something, and your self-esteem level—the belief that you are worth doing what you want to do. Doing a better job of leading those voices leads to more effective behavior, which in business would translate into higher productivity, higher morale, and folks who stay in their jobs longer. In organizational terminology, this means lower turnover and higher revenues, all based on how we manage the voices in our head. There aren't many training programs that directly address this element.

Wright

You mentioned helping people achieve success and leadership "with intention." Is there a way to do it by accident?

Wofford

These are two courses we provide—"Leadership Intentionally" and "Success Intentionally." Believe it or not, there are people who stumble on the right path to success by accident. They make it big, become successful, and make their way without really giving much thought to how they have done it.

If people are not aware of how they achieved such a success, the process becomes difficult to repeat. If you were to ask a random seven out of ten people how they achieved their success, many of them (based on my experience) would say "hard work" or "I'm not sure" or "I got lucky" or "from the support of a higher power." None of these answers are necessarily incorrect, but they take the control of achieving success out of the achiever's hands.

I believe we have far more control or influence than most take credit for. Others, who observe people whom they believe are successful often say, "They are an overnight success! They must be lucky!" when in fact, those people probably had been making their way toward their success for years.

Yet, until one can actually identify what skills, attributes, talents, and desires got them to that point of success it's difficult to duplicate it. This is why so many people have one big pivotal moment or pivotal milestone or success in their life. They're not sure how they got there—did they get there on purpose or intentionally? So duplicating that process becomes confusing and often unattainable. The Success Intentionally training we provide imparts the knowledge to participants of how to:

- Get out of their own way of success and overcome internal barriers,
- Uncover what was helpful when they were successful in the past, and
- Then help them map out a process that will allow them to repeat their own success and eliminate personal barriers that might be standing in the way of their own progress.

Wright
What exactly does it take to be successful?

Wofford
What exactly is your personal definition of success? That is the question that reveals the attributes it will take to get there. Based on your own definition, it can take many different things.

If we were to look at the foundational elements of success for most people, they often have some tie to financial success or status or promotion to a higher level position at the office. If they're in business working with other people, they might seek notoriety—for some, success means celebrity status. Success for everyone is different and the key factors are: the *skills* you need to get where you consider to be successful, the *desire* to get there, and even more importantly, the willingness to sacrifice what it might take to get there.

As we all know, success is not necessarily an easy road; there are usually difficult choices and sacrifices. This is why many people, halfway toward their goal or even right up to achievement, say, "This is too hard. I'll just go back to doing something that's easier and settle for mediocrity." Now, they may never use the word "mediocrity," but this is what they choose because it is easier. And if they choose the easy road, they never achieve the dreams or success or big ideas they might have had that would have defined their life in their own mind as successful.

This is why, before we begin to coach or train participants, we help them map out exactly what they want with our *Success . . . Intentionally Making Dreams Happen Manual.* This workbook gives participants a chance to get clear on *what* they want or their desires, and then we can help them identify what skills they might need to acquire or improve upon to get there more quickly.

Wright

Can anyone use this formula to achieve his or her own desired success?

Wofford

Absolutely. The key is that not everyone, as we mentioned, will maintain the burning desire to achieve their own success. For some that could mean the pinnacle, perfect corporate job. For others, success may have nothing to do with work, a paycheck, or a W-2. One could be successful and never leave his or her home and family. One could be successful creating a career or a livelihood out of what others would consider junk.

A gentleman I know has made a huge financial, personally successful, and fulfilling career out of recycling chicken manure—something, I might add, most would not be willing to do. In this case, it's a dirty job and someone didn't *have* to do it, he chose to do it and do it well; but there are obvious sacrifices.

There are just so many definitions of success that anyone could apply the formula we provide, acquire the necessary skills, and achieve success as that person defines it.

Wright

Well, he just found a need and filled it didn't he?

Wofford

That he did. He found a need and filled it and has done amazing things with it. And we all have that ability if we will just get out of our own way. We all have what I call internal skills, gifts, and talents. It's whether or not we choose to use them and whether or not we're able to identify those people, things, or voices that are acting as barriers to our own achievement.

Wright

Tell me more about the CORE profile and how this is used to help people with their achievements.

Wofford

The CORE profile was developed by Dr. Sherry Buffington and her daughter, Gina Morgan. This dynamic duo has conducted twenty years of research with thousands of participants using the CORE Multi-Dimensional Awareness Profile and other tools in the CORE profile system.

Dr. Buffington, as many of us, had been subjected to the categorical delivery of results from tools such as the Myers Briggs Testing Indicator (MBTI), DISC Profile, CARE Profile, Wilson Profile, and several others. What these tools most often provide, on any given day in a multitude of different situations, is a high degree of inaccuracy, much of which comes not from the tool itself, but from the facilitation of the results.

The CORE tool is different partly because it has a 92 percent accuracy track record in identifying how someone is wired. In addition, it creates the expectation that with this information you will grow and shows you how to do that. It also allows for and tracks growth in the following three areas:

1. How we perceive ourselves. (Many other profiling tools also provide this and then leave you with your own perceptions, which we all know can be dead wrong.)
2. How we function on a daily basis, which often is quite different than how we think we are doing.
3. How we perform under different degrees of stress on an average day. Stress is so much a part of our daily lives that this part of the profile becomes instrumental in assessing what skills are missing or undeveloped for many people, and where they would benefit from further training.

Other profiles do not provide that level of in-depth knowledge. Other profiles use a snapshot approach, based on your own perception. David, have you ever perceived yourself to be one way and someone else saw you as some other way? Have you ever been in a great mood and seen your world through rose colored glasses one day and then been in a bad mood and seen the world in a warped fashion the next?

Wright

Absolutely.

Wofford

Of course—we all do. Our perceptions can be warped. They can be inaccurate and they can be downright wrong, depending on the situation that we're in. With CORE's three-dimensional process, as opposed to the one-dimensional information many other profiles provide, you are able to go beyond a one-time snapshot and see yourself in video. Life is a moving progression, not a one time snapshot. If we were all the same all the time and growth were no option, then these other profiles would suffice. CORE gives you enough information to grow on and even provides a mechanism in Part 3 to track and measure that growth. CEOs like this tool a great deal because it gives them the ability to measure elements such as training, coaching, and personal development.

CORE also indicates how well developed you are in the four original temperaments upon which almost all profiles are based, originally discovered by Hippocrates and further explored by Carl Jung. These temperaments have many labels depending on the tool you are using. In CORE, they are called Commander, Organizer, Entertainer, and Relater. These four allow us to look at your development level in terms of "getting things done," "getting things right," "getting appreciated," and "getting along with others," the four driving forces behind each temperament. What becomes important about these temperaments is that the more well developed you are in each of them, the higher your emotional intelligence is. A recent Herman Trends Report revealed emotional intelligence as an 86 percent predictor of success.

But there's more. If you're well developed in Commander skills, Organizer skills, and Relater skills, as well as Entertainer skills, then your overall ability to relate with others, your ability to handle stress, your ability to deal with change, and your ability to build relationships is immeasurably increased.

Success is said to be attributed to one's ability to relate to and work with others well. CORE gives you the very information about what may be standing in your way of success and working well with others. A lack of development in one temperament can make all the difference. In addition, if the way you perceive yourself is different than the way you are functioning, this too can get in your way. The information we receive from a simple forty-minute online profile is fascinating and what we hear most often from people when we facilitate the results is, "Wow, how did you know? I have been trying to work on that for years and you just gave me the secret. Thank you!"

Wright

How is this different from any number of other profiles in the marketplace?

Wofford

Other than the three parts I mentioned David, so many other profiles portray a negative image of one's weaknesses. The focus is not on your strengths or where you gain your energy. The reality is that we all have a natural leaning toward one temperament or another. It isn't right or wrong, it just is. If the facilitator of your results on your profile is wired one way and you are showing up as wired another, the message can be one of "you must change."

In addition, other profiles are a picture of who you are today. No more and no less. They seem to leave little room for change or little encouragement that you can grow, change, and develop. In fact, many of my coaching clients tell me this has been the only tool that actually tells people what they can *do* with the information, rather than just providing a label.

Let's take the Myers Briggs, for example. This tool has been widely accepted, used and misused, interpreted and misinterpreted, and even proved inaccurate in many ways by experts in this industry. It gives a picture of what you're doing today, the mood you are in today, and leaves out some fundamental pieces of who you are and how you actually function, versus how you perceive yourself and what those actions do to you on an average day when stress increases. In other words, it does not reveal how your natural strengths or underdeveloped attributes show up when you are relating with others.

For example David, if I took a picture of you with a camera, you would have one outfit on that day. If you never changed clothes, you never changed your mood, and you never had a bad day, then the picture I took of you that day would always be accurate. When you take a Myers Briggs or a DISC profile, that picture of you on the day you took the profile would show results that would be accurate for that day. If you never changed anything, those results would be absolutely accurate. What CORE provides in Part 3 is the development of where you are the day you took the CORE assessment. When you retake the profile on Part 3, called a "Progress Report," you would see an abbreviated version of the entire profile, and your progress or growth. We can show you where you are today, so that you know at the beginning "this is where I am today," and then show you where you have grown over time—usually three, six, or nine months later. Your progress will show up on Part 3 and you would be able to see the measurable value of your work and effort and the development of you.

The CORE assessment tool is invaluable because it allows us to show organizations the value or return on investment of their training dollars when we specifically provide training to improve under-developed areas.

Wright

What kind of effect has this information had on your life?

Wofford

It has had an amazing effect on my life. I have taken and been a believer for a long time in the Myers Briggs Testing Indicator, as well as DISC and a few others. What I have been told by people who have analyzed my Myers Briggs results is that there were some attributes I needed to change, frankly, in order to be accepted into human existence. That is not something a person wants to hear: "Okay, here's your label and parts of you are wrong. Now, in order for you to be acceptable you must change X, Y, and Z right away." Of course, I am sure that not all MBTI facilitators take this approach, yet the underlying message of the information seems to lean that way.

When I took the CORE profile I had a tremendous amount of trepidation about what I was going to be told. I was concerned that if I didn't score a certain number or certain value on the questions, that my behavior was not going to be "right" or "correct." What I found instead was that at no time did the CORE facilitator tell me I was wrong or anything short of just fine the way I was. There was no, "This is what you must change" or "This is what's wrong with you" or "This is what you have to do different." What I was told was, "These are the areas in which you are well developed, "These are the areas in which you may want to look into developing some additional strategy, additional techniques, and additional skills in," and "Here are some ideas for more development" (e.g., a training class, a book, or finding a mentor or role model to help you gain more skill in a particular area).

There's nothing wrong with any of us in these developmental areas. It's a matter of being well developed or not well developed. It only stands to reason that the area in which we are naturally gifted or naturally wired would be more well developed, much like those who have been right-handed all their life and were born that way are going to be better at being right-handed than those who are left-handed and who had only recently begun to practice being right-handed or frankly, someone who has been doing it unnaturally most of his or her life. The person might be good, but it will never be "natural" for him or her.

When my CORE results were facilitated by a coach (and this is the preferred method of results delivery), rather than receiving a report, I was given a direction and suggestions about where I could develop more skill and therefore gain more energy around what I was doing. I was not treated judgmentally and it allowed me to keep an open mind during the process.

There is no judgment passed in the facilitation of CORE because of the simple fact that we will be better at what we naturally prefer and lesser developed in those skills we either don't use or are not naturally comfortable with. Rather than try to make people fit into a desired norm, CORE allows people to be okay with who they are and even begin to like who they are and learn where they get their greatest energy. CORE also creates interest in learning skills in each temperament so that you can increase your tool kit and relate more effectively with all types of people.

Going back to your original question David, personally, CORE has given me permission to like the Commander traits that I posses without constantly being judged as too overbearing or falling in the female witch category. It has also afforded me far greater interest in developing more Relater traits and Entertainer traits so that I can be stronger in working well with everyone out there instead of just my favorite commander colleagues.

The amount of freedom that this tool has given me and the boost it has given me in my own confidence and self-esteem is hard to explain, but I can tell you what others are saying: "Monica, you seem so much happier and comfortable with the person you are." That is the highest compliment I think I have ever received and it is all due to my experience with the CORE tool. And to think I had spent thousands on seminars and books to fix who I was all these years. I wish I had found CORE a decade ago.

Wright
Can anyone become a leader with this information?

Wofford

That depends. My qualifications for someone to become a leader are that he or she has the desire, skills, and is willing to practice.

It also significantly depends on what kind of people one is leading. If you wish to lead a group of Organizers and you posses too little or no development in the skills this temperament provides, then leading them will be difficult if for no other reason than the "language" barrier. You and the group you want to lead in this case will not have a common ground from which to relate and on which to build rapport.

If someone wants to lead folks who need a hands-on manager, who value people, and who nurture them and yet that person lives solely in well developed Commander land and that person's primary focus is on tasks, then this may be a challenging leadership environment. At the very least (and this happens a lot) the group will have a lot of employee complaints, a high turnover, and will need more damage control than a group in which the leader and members understand each other.

When I wrote *Contagious Leadership,* I spoke about this concept of understanding each other, along with nine other attributes and skills of an effective leader. David, a lot of these attributes center around leading the voices in your own head more effectively before attempting to lead, guide, motivate, and direct others. CORE can help you not only understand, but lead the voices in your head more effectively. If a person is willing to do that and willing to practice developing more traits than the ones they are naturally wired to do well, then yes, the person can use this information to become a leader.

Wright

Are you saying I talk to myself more than anybody else does?

Wofford

I think so, but I don't know. Do you talk to yourself David? David, are you there? Finish that conversation in your head and then let me know.

Wright

I'm glad you said that. I feel a lot better this morning. I thought there was something wrong with me.

Wofford

No—I ask rooms full of hundreds of people on a regular basis in seminars the same question. I ask them all, "How many of you talk to yourself?" and I get a wide variety of hands raised in the room. The folks who are not raising their hand I will look at and say, "Now those who have not raised their hand are probably sitting there thinking, "I don't know, do I talk to myself? I'm not real sure." That always gets a great chuckle because the reality is, good grief, we all talk to ourselves all the time. It's not the talking that's the problem, it's what we say that is a problem.

Jack Canfield, co-author of *Chicken Soup for the Soul,* was a psychotherapist for many years before he wrote that book, and during that time he discovered a statistic regarding how we talk to ourselves. It is a scary thing, but most people say fourteen negative things for every single positive thing said.

If the leader you are attempting to be is someone who can rally motivation and gather the troops around, inspiring them to grow and perform, and yet your focus is more on the negativity around you and if the voices in your head are saying, "I can't do this, I can't get it all done today, I'm overwhelmed, I'm a looser, I'm not good at my job" or whatever the case may be, the bottom line is you will fail. If you are saying the opposite—something like, "I am supervisor hear me roar," then those voices are guiding your behavior too and that is going to rub off on every single one of the folks you have the privilege of leading. In other words, either way won't work.

Wright

Can anyone become a leader with this information?

Wofford

Anyone has the ability to lead. As I briefly mentioned earlier, in my opinion, leadership is comprised of skill, desire, and practice. If one does not have the desire, it's very hard to force him or her to be a leader. So if people have the desire to lead, whether they are leading a grass roots movement, leading a political party, leading a country, leading a group of retail sales associates, or leading an entire fortune 500 company, that desire is the first internal kernel of truth they have to come to grips with. Once they have the desire, we can provide them with the skills and even walk them through and coach them through the practice process.

Wright

What success stories have you seen emerge from the training sessions you do in the area of success and leadership?

Wofford

How much time do you have?

Wright

You can even help *me?*

Wofford

Absolutely—I can even help you. We, being Monica Wofford International, Inc, have conducted training with companies like Hormel Foods, DSM Pharmaceuticals, the U.S. Mint, Estée Lauder, Cingular Wireless, and the Las Vegas Hilton. I've also conducted public seminars in which Coca-Cola has been involved and Astra Zeneca employees have participated.

What we have found through success stories, testimonials, and letters sent to our organization is that breaking leadership down to your basic ten steps, making it easy for folks to listen to the information, and immediately apply it to their daily personal and professional lives works. They are telling us over and over that the seminar and the CORE information have changed the way they lead other people, as well as the voices in their head.

As an example, I had a client who worked with me when she was a part of the Hallmark Card Company. Her team was struggling with building trust and the reality that people, as they are in many organizations, were now having to do the job of two to three people instead of the one job they were used to. We're talking about a high stress, high change, fast deadlines, and lots of high client demands environment.

What we discovered after completing the seminar and talking with her further is that a few simple changes in her communication style (a key to effective leadership), minor modifications in her delivery of direction (another key to effective leadership), and a conscious awareness that she needed to lead by example—those elements of trust, core respect-building, and confidence—she was able to take a team that was ready to quit and turn those team members into a cohesive, unified group of people who to this day rely on each other more so than they ever have in their history to get the job done. They are turning deadlines around before they're due as opposed to asking forgiveness later for missing them.

It is amazing to watch and a great success story.

Wright

What would you say is the key difference between what you provide in your training and presentations and that of other success or leadership speakers and trainers?

Wofford

What is different is our ability, through the use of the CORE tool, to measure the results that we promise in our training programs. Training measurement and proof of an ROI is often the most difficult element to measure, yet we have found a way. In addition, our training is created out of true need and an assessment of these needs, as opposed to "drive-by" training events that merely motivate for a moment and are then forgotten.

This isn't your run-of-the-mill, fix-the-world-in-a-day training firm. In fact, we turn clients away if we don't feel we can provide them with the results they are looking for. At the same time, we significantly help clients reduce their turnover numbers and increase revenues through skill and knowledge transfer (also known as training). We recently saved an organization 2.64 million dollars by helping to reduce their turnover rate from 142 percent to 78 percent. Those are the kinds of results we can prove that make us different from other success or leadership speakers and trainers.

David, speakers and trainers who work within Monica Wofford International, Inc. (myself included), spend a tremendous amount of time on the front end before the engagement ever begins in uncovering what the true needs of a client are. We seek to ensure that we have a connection with the client and that there's a good fit for all involved. We look to be the right fit for a client and that the client is the right fit for our organization.

For many clients we employ the CORE tool to assess the needs and determine areas of focus. This results in specific training that meets the needs of those involved. Once we've delivered the training, most of which is completely customized (though we also offer "off-the-shelf" programs), we return with the CORE profile tool and measure the development of those who have been trained. This follow-up process can occur in thirty days, sixty days, ninety days, or six months after the training class. What we are able to do with Part 3 of the

CORE tool is show the client on a hard copy graph, with numbers, the "proof of the pudding" in their return of their training investment.

There are quite a few things that set us apart, David, and they make us different. While not costing the client an arm and a leg more than any of the other alternatives, we provide results that are dramatically different and, in our opinion, far more effective. Our customers repeatedly tell us that our services have proven to be far more effective than many other training sessions they have experienced before.

Wright

What a great conversation. You've given me a lot to think about as well.

Wofford

I'm glad, David.

Wright

Today we've been talking with Monica Wofford. Monica, thank you so much for being with us today and for taking all this time to answer all these questions. Thank you for being with us on *Speaking of Success.*

Wofford

My pleasure, David. Now, go out there and be successful on purpose, but keep a close ear on those voices in your head, okay?

About the Author

MONICA WOFFORD is a nationally acclaimed speaker, author, trainer, and leadership expert with more than seventeen years of experience. She has written, among other books, *Contagious Leadership*, which was complimented by Vice President Dick Cheney. Her areas of expertise include Leadership and Success both being achieved with intention and on purpose. Corporations often call on Monica to teach their managers how to swim in the deep end of the corporate pool when all they were given was a promotion and a life jacket, but no new leadership skills. Monica's speaking and training career began back in 1989 and has taken her to all fifty states and several countries. She is known for engaging audiences and helping them make radical shifts in the behavior that creates successful leaders, whether of their own lives or the lives of others. Monica's training influences and produces results in the leadership of employees, customers, and even the voices in your head!

Monica Wofford
Monica Wofford International
P.O. Box 683316
Orlando, FL 32868
Phone: 866.382.0121
E-mail: Monica@Monicawofford.com
www.monicawofford.com